MONSTER HUNTERS

FINDING WEREWOLVES

By Therese Shea

Gareth Stevens
PUBLISHING

Please visit our website, www.garethstevens.com. For a free color catalog of all our high-quality books, call toll free 1-800-542-2595 or fax 1-877-542-2596.

Library of Congress Cataloging-in-Publication Data
Names: Shea, Therese, author.
Title: Finding werewolves / Therese Shea.
Description: New York : Gareth Stevens Publishing, [2026] | Series: Monster hunters | Includes index.
Identifiers: LCCN 2024061406 (print) | LCCN 2024061407 (ebook) | ISBN 9781482472202 (library binding) | ISBN 9781482472196 (paperback) | ISBN 9781482472219 (ebook)
Subjects: LCSH: Werewolves–Juvenile literature.
Classification: LCC GR830.W4 S543 2026 (print) | LCC GR830.W4 (ebook) | DDC 398.24/54–dc23/eng/20250208
LC record available at https://lccn.loc.gov/2024061406
LC ebook record available at https://lccn.loc.gov/2024061407

Published in 2026 by
Gareth Stevens Publishing
2544 Clinton Street
Buffalo, NY 14224

Designer: Andrea Davison-Bartolotta
Editor: Therese Shea

Photo credits: Cover, pp. 1, 24 Shutterstock AI/Shutterstock.com; cover, p. 1, series art (glowing compass rose) LoveDesignShop/Shutterstock.com; series art (cardinal compass rose) Angela Ksen/Shutterstock.com; series art (ordinal compass rose) jame05/Shutterstock.com; series art (fact box rope border) LanaN/Shutterstock.com; series art (fact box wood) EE SPACE/Shutterstock.com; series art (map background) Olha Andreichyn/Shutterstock.com; series art (curled paper background) MIGUEL G. SAAVEDRA/Shutterstock.com; series art (flat paper) Paladin12/Shutterstock.com; p. 5 (fur texture) Binimin/Shutterstock.com; p. 5 (main) Declan Hillman/Shutterstock.com; p. 6 Tollaru/Shutterstock.com; p. 7 (background) Tan_supa/Shutterstock.com; p. 7 (main) Los Angeles County Museum of Art; p. 8 QuirkCraft Studio/Shutterstock.com; p. 9 Lefteris Penteli/Shutterstock.com; p. 9 gt29/Shutterstock.com; p. 11 (top) File:Ring21.jpg/Wikimedia Commons; p. 11 (bottom) File:Tullstorpstenen, DR 271, Tullstorp 1- 1, Runristning.jpg/Wikimedia Commons; p. 13 (background) Arnaldur Sigurdarson/Shutterstock.com; pp. 13, 15 (map) Andrei Minsk/Shutterstock.com; p. 15 (bottom background) DanieleGay/Shutterstock.com; p. 15 (top background) VHarasymiv/Shutterstock.com; p. 17 (background) The Metropolitan Museum of Art; p. 17 (main) File:WeirdTalesv36n2pg038 The Werewolf Howls.png/Wikimedia Commons; p. 19 (background) Furiarossa/Shutterstock.com; p. 19 (maps) Sarfaraz82/Shutterstock.com; p. 20 Gary Riegel/Shutterstock.com; p. 21 Joe Dordo Brnobic/Shutterstock.com; p. 23 (inset) File:Tepeyóllotl 1.jpg/Wikimedia Commons; p. 23 (jaguar) Zaruba Ondrej/Shutterstock.com; p. 23 (map) Peter Hermes Furian/Shutterstock.com; p. 25 File:PetrusGonsalvus.jpg/Wikimedia Commons; p. 27 (top) Cinematic/Alamy Stock Photo; p. 27 (bottom) Sarunyu L/Shutterstock.com; pp. 28, 29 (map) Janos Levente/Shutterstock.com; pp. 28, 29 (paper) AKaiser/Shutterstock.com.

Printed in the United States of America

CPSIA compliance information: Batch #CSGS26: For further information contact Gareth Stevens at 1-800-542-2595.

CONTENTS

Words in the glossary appear in **bold** type the first time they are used in the text.

WEREWOLF HUNT!

Imagine you're outside on a warm, clear night. You look up and see a beautiful full moon. Nice, right? But then you hear howling nearby. Is that the neighbor's dog? Next, you hear some rustling leaves. A hairy face and claws pop out of the bushes. Finally, you see the sharp teeth. It's a werewolf!

Werewolf tales have been passed down for hundreds of years. Is there any truth to them? It's your job to find out. Grab some maps of the world, and get ready to track some werewolves!

In an early form of the English language called Old English, "wer" or "were" meant "man," so werewolf meant "man-wolf."

COMMON WEREWOLF FEATURES

- Turns into werewolf only during the full moon
- Turns into a werewolf at night and back to human during the day
- Turns into werewolf after being bitten by another werewolf
- If wounded, will have the wound as a werewolf and as a human
- May look like a wolf or half-wolf, half-human
- May stand on two legs
- May be killed by burning, by being shot with a silver bullet, or by drinking vinegar

Werewolves have different features in different tales. Here are some of the most common.

LYCAON'S PUNISHMENT

Tales of men becoming wolves go back thousands of years! An early **myth** comes from ancient Greece.

Zeus, the king of the gods, visited the king of Arcadia, who was named Lycaon. Lycaon tried to trick Zeus to see how powerful Zeus was. Zeus didn't like being tested. He became so angry at Lycaon that he turned the king into a wolf. However, Lycaon never turned back to a man, as werewolves do in modern tales.

Behind the Myth

The Arcadian king's name is related to the Greek word for "wolf"—*lykos*.

This **engraving**, from 1589, shows Zeus (left) turning Lycaon (right) into a wolf.

Greece is a country in southern Europe. Arcadia, Lycaon's ancient kingdom, is still a **region** of Greece today. Let's find it with your maps and map skills.

Use the compass rose. It's the tool on the map that shows the four main directions, called cardinal directions: north (N), south (S), east (E), and west (W). First, look in southern Greece for the Peloponnese **peninsula**. Arcadia is an area on the Peloponnese, which is nearly surrounded by the Mediterranean Sea.

Most of ancient Arcadia was mountainous.
Today's Arcadia is a bit larger than the ancient kingdom of Lycaon.
GREECE
ARCADIA
N
W
E
S

THE STORY OF SIGMUND AND SINFJOTLI

Other ancient people had werewolf-like myths too. The Germanic people of Northern Europe had their own tales, such as the *Volsunga* ***Saga***.

In one story, Sigmund and his son Sinfjotli (SIN-fyawt-lee) came upon several sleeping men in wolf skins. They put on the wolf skins but discovered they couldn't take them off. The magic wolf skins turned them into wolves. After 10 days, they were able to take off the skins and turn back into men. They burned the wolf skins in a fire.

Sigmund, shown here, and Sinfjotli had many adventures together.

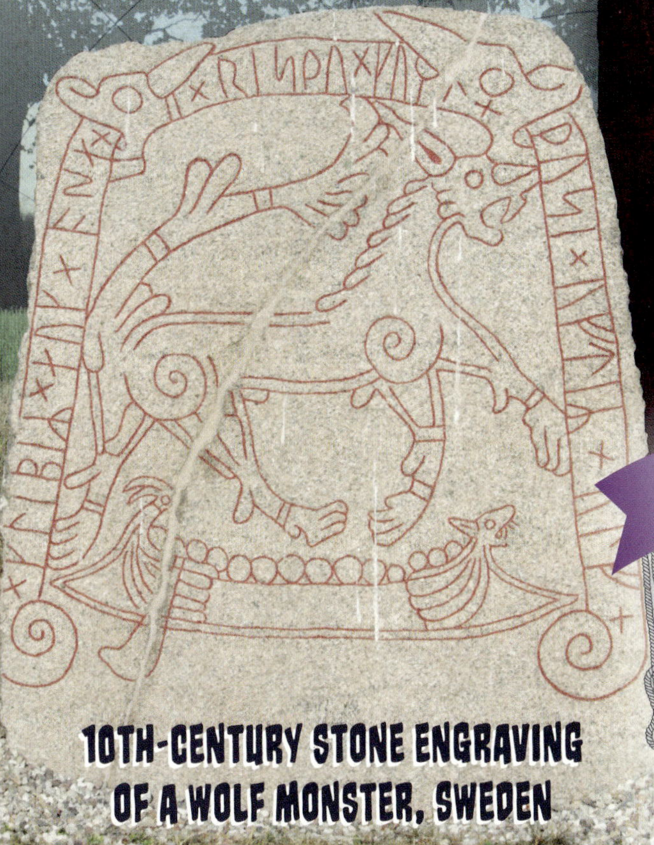

10TH-CENTURY STONE ENGRAVING OF A WOLF MONSTER, SWEDEN

Behind the Myth

As werewolves, Sigmund and Sinfjotli were fierce. They killed many men. Sigmund even wounded Sinfjotli, who was only saved when a raven dropped a magic healing leaf.

The *Volsunga Saga* was first written down in the Icelandic language more than 800 years ago. Let's head to Iceland to **investigate** its origins.

Iceland is located in the North Atlantic Ocean. Greenland is to its west. Norway is to its east. Check these directions using the compass rose.

The author of the saga, who is unknown, knew a lot about Scandinavian myths and used them in their tales. Scandinavia is the term used to refer to the **cultures** in Norway, Sweden, and Denmark. The seafaring warriors called the Vikings likely brought Scandinavian myths to Iceland.

Iceland is considered a part of Europe.

Iceland has about 200 **volcanoes** as well as glaciers, or large sheets of slowly moving ice.

WEREWOLVES IN FRANCE

We'll need to head to France for our next investigation. The tales you'll read aren't myths, but you can decide how true they sound.

France is a European country. It's southeast of Iceland. "Southeast" is called an ordinal, or intercardinal, direction. It's exactly between south and east on a compass rose. Northeast (NE), southwest (SW), and northwest (NW) are also ordinal directions. The compass rose on the map of France on the next page includes both cardinal and ordinal directions.

France is in Western Europe. Most of France is flat plains, but it has mountains in its southern and eastern regions. Wolves in the Vosges mountains in the east inspired werewolf tales.

Behind the Myth

In French tales, the werewolf is called *loup-garou* (loo-ga-roo).

In the 1500s, several French men reported turning into werewolves. They all said they had special **ointments** that they rubbed on themselves that caused them to change. They were accused of, or charged with, attacking people. One of the men, Giles Garnier, was found guilty of lycanthropy, or turning into a werewolf, as well as witchcraft.

No one knows if these men really believed they were werewolves or just used that as an excuse for their bad actions. They may have been falsely accused too. Whatever the reason, the stories made Europeans fear werewolves.

Behind the Myth

A lycanthrope ("wolf-human," in Greek) is another name for a werewolf.

There were many werewolf **trials** in the Middle Ages. Some of the accused may have been forced to say they were werewolves.

GERMANY'S FAMOUS WEREWOLF

Peter Stubbe lived in the town of Bedburg, in today's eastern Germany. He was accused of being a werewolf in 1589. He was blamed for killings in the area. Hunters said they saw him transform, or change. He said he had a magic belt that caused the transformation. That belt was never found, though.

Stubbe may have been forced to confess his guilt. Some think he was blamed because he was disliked or different from others in his community. He may have been blamed because people needed an explanation for scary events in Bedburg.

A map's scale is a tool that tells you real-life distances. On this map, the scale says 1 inch on the map is equal to about 60 miles in real life. So, Bedburg is about 60 miles (97 km) from the Netherlands' border.

AFRICAN TALES

Even places that don't have wolves have similar myths. Tales of people turning into hyenas are told in several places in Africa. In some stories, it's the opposite—hyenas **disguise** themselves as people.

Cultures in Cameroon, Chad, and Sudan have tales of half-hyena, half-people too. Locate these countries on the map.

Africa is the **continent** south of Europe. Somalia is the easternmost African country. Do you see it on the map? There, some people talk of the Qori-ismaris, a man who could turn himself into a half-man, half-hyena with a magic stick.

Behind the Myth

Tales of hyena-people may have been a way to keep children from wandering in the wilderness where animals such as hyenas could hurt them.

In Ethiopia, a country just west of Somalia, "were-hyena" are called *bouda*, or *buda*. Many outsiders were accused of being *bouda*.

Hyenas are fast, dangerous, and hungry animals.

NORTH AMERICAN CRYPTIDS

There have been reports of half-human, half-animal creatures in the Americas. So, head west across the Atlantic Ocean to learn more about these cryptids. That's the name for animals that have been claimed, but not proven, to exist.

The ancient Olmec culture of Mexico created art that reflected the "were-jaguar," a humanlike jaguar. The jaguar is the biggest cat in the Americas. Hundreds of years later, the Aztec people of the same region worshipped a humanlike jaguar god named Tepeyollotli.

Mesoamerica is a region that stretches from southern North America to the western coast of Central America. It was the home of several important ancient Native cultures.

TEPEYOLLOTLI

JAGUAR

SOME WEREWOLF MYSTERIES SOLVED?

So, do you believe in werewolves? There are some real explanations in science for werewolf features and actions. For example, people with a rare condition called clinical lycanthropy think they have turned into an animal or can turn into an animal.

Behind the Myth

Other people may have eaten or drunk something that made them **hallucinate** and think they turned into werewolves.

In addition, rabies is a disease, or illness, that can cause people to want to bite other people in extreme cases. Another condition, hypertrichosis, causes unusual hair growth all over the body, including the face. Could people with clinical lycanthropy, rabies, or hypertrichosis have been accused of being werewolves? It's likely!

Petrus Gonsalvus (1537-1618) was a noble who likely had hypertrichosis in the court of King Henry II of France.

WEREWOLVES IN POPULAR CULTURE

People are so interested in the idea of werewolves that they often pop up as characters in modern fiction books, movies, and TV shows. The *Harry Potter* books and movies included both good and evil werewolves. The *Twilight* series featured werewolves too. The *Hotel Transylvania* movies had many funny werewolf characters.

Werewolves are a key role in popular board games, card games, and video games. Why do you think werewolves and other were-creatures have remained such a lasting part of cultures?

Actor Lon Cheney Jr. played the title role in the famous and wildly popular 1941 movie *The Wolf Man*.

WERE-CREATURES AROUND THE WORLD

There are many stories of half-animal, half-human creatures around the world. Continue your journey!

GLOSSARY

continent: One of the seven great landmasses on Earth.

culture: The beliefs and ways of life of a group of people.

disguise: To have a false appearance.

engraving: Words or shapes cut into a surface, such as stone.

hallucinate: To seem to see, hear, feel, or smell something that does not exist.

investigate: To search in an orderly way for facts about something.

myth: A story that was told by a people to explain a practice, belief, or natural event.

ointment: A thick substance put on skin, usually to aid a condition or injury.

peninsula: A narrow piece of land that extends into water from the mainland.

region: A large area of land that has features that make it different from nearby areas of land.

saga: A long story or account of heroic adventures or historical events.

trial: A legal process to decide if someone is guilty of a crime.

volcano: An opening in a planet's surface through which hot, liquid rock sometimes flows.

FOR MORE INFORMATION

Books

Anderhagen, Anna. *The Science of Werewolves*. Minneapolis, MN: A&D Xtreme, 2024.

Gleason, Carrie. *Guide to Werewolves*. New York, NY: Crabtree Publishing Company, 2023.

Phillips-Bartlett, Rebecca. *Werewolves*. Minneapolis, MN: Bearport Publishing Company, 2025.

Websites

Gray Wolf
kids.nationalgeographic.com/animals/mammals/facts/gray-wolf
Read more about wolves, and think about how they may have inspired the legend of the werewolf.

Werewolf
kids.britannica.com/kids/article/werewolf/600679
Review this cryptid's features in Britannica Kids.

Werewolf Facts for Kids
kids.kiddle.co/Werewolf
Learn more werewolf myths from around the world.

Publisher's note to educators and parents: Our editors have carefully reviewed these websites to ensure that they are suitable for students. Many websites change frequently, however, and we cannot guarantee that a site's future contents will continue to meet our high standards of quality and educational value. Be advised that students should be closely supervised whenever they access the internet.

INDEX